Animal Ears

By Connor Stratton

level 2
little blue readers

www.littlebluehousebooks.com

Little Blue House is distributed by North Star Editions:
sales@northstareditions.com | 888-417-0195

Produced for Little Blue House by Red Line Editorial.

Photographs ©: iStockphoto, cover, 4, 7 (top), 7 (bottom), 11 (top), 11 (bottom), 12, 15 (top), 15 (bottom), 18, 21, 22–23, 24 (top left), 24 (top right), 24 (bottom left), 24 (bottom right); Shutterstock Images, 9 (top), 9 (bottom), 16–17

Library of Congress Control Number: 2020900813

ISBN
978-1-64619-174-1 (hardcover)
978-1-64619-208-3 (paperback)
978-1-64619-276-2 (ebook pdf)
978-1-64619-242-7 (hosted ebook)

Printed in the United States of America
Mankato, MN
082020

About the Author

Connor Stratton enjoys spotting new animals and writing books for children. He lives in Minnesota.

Table of Contents

Kinds of Ears **5**

Big and Small **13**

Ears Everywhere **19**

Glossary **24**

Index **24**

Kinds of Ears

Many animals have
two ears.
Their ears are on
their heads.
Ears help animals hear.

Different animals' ears look different.

Some ears stick up.

Other ears hang down.

Ears often face forward.
Some ears can
move back.

Animals can have hairy ears.

Squirrels can have hairy ears.

Cats can have hairy ears too.

Big and Small

Some animals have
big ears.
Elephants have the
biggest ears on Earth.

Gorillas are big.

But these animals have small ears.

Bats are small.

But these animals have big ears.

15

Seals have small ears.

Their ears are just holes.

Seals can hear

underwater.

They can hear out of

the water too.

Ears Everywhere

Animals with ears

are everywhere.

Camels have ears.

Camels live in the desert.

Goats have ears.

Goats live in

the mountains.

Monkeys have ears.

Monkeys live in the rain forest.

Glossary

bat

monkey

elephant

squirrel

Index

C
cats, 10

G
gorillas, 14

E
elephants, 13

S
seals, 16